Can You See What I See?
SEYMOUR
AND THE JUICE BOX BOAT
WALTER WICK

SCHOLASTIC INC.
New York   Toronto   London   Auckland   Sydney   Mexico City
New Delhi   Hong Kong   Buenos Aires

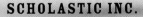

ISBN 0-439-67848-X

Published by Scholastic Inc.

SCHOLASTIC, CARTWHEEL BOOKS,

and associated logos are trademarks

and/or registered trademarks of Scholastic Inc.

12 11 10 9 8 7 6 5 4 3 2 1   4 5 6 7 8 9/0

Printed in the U.S.A. 40

First Scholastic paperback printing, October 2004

Acknowledgments

Special thanks to Dan Helt and Kim Wildey for their
assistance in the studio; to Linda Cheverton-Wick for
her inspiration; to Rich Deas for his book design;
and to Grace Maccarone for her editorial guidance.

FOR LINDA

Can you see a turtle,

 scissors,

2 spools?

 Can you see Seymour

with a cart full of tools?

Can you see a bunny,

 a barn,

a cow?

 Can you see a pig?

Where's Seymour now?

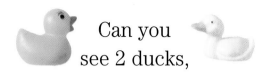 Can you
see 2 ducks,

a pencil that's red?

 Can you help
Seymour

find some thread?

 Can you see
an elephant,

a bunny with a bow,

  2 bears,

a clothespin?

Where did Seymour go?

Can you see a frog,

 a button that's round,

2 teapots,

and the ladder

that Seymour found?

Can you see a straw,

 an ice-cream treat,

a tiger's tail,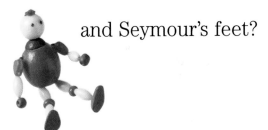

and Seymour's feet?

Can you see
an anchor,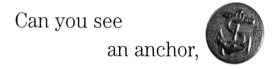

 a truck,

4 trees?

Can you see the saw

 that Seymour sees?

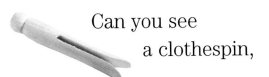
Can you see
a clothespin,

3 pigs,

a cow?

Can you see
what Seymour
is doing right now?

Can you see
a starfish,

 a crab,

a ray?

 Can you see
Seymour...

. . . sail away?

FOR MORE LEARNING FUN

In this picture adventure story, written and photographed by Walter Wick, a little toy boy wants to take a journey in a boat he makes from an ordinary juice box! You and your child will enjoy helping Seymour find and collect all the things he needs to make this special boat... and wondering where the boat will take him. The discussion questions help your child build vocabulary, notice picture details, and more!

Pages 8–9: *Can you see a yellow car and yellow blocks? Can you see other yellow things?*

Pages 10–11: *Cows and pigs are farm animals. Can you see other kinds of animals?*

Pages 12–13: *Can you see four red arches? Can you see other shapes?*

Pages 14–15: *Seymour's name begins with the letter S. Can you see the letter S?*

Pages 16–17: *Can you see 2 stars? 2 marbles? 2 blue arches?*

Pages 18–19: *Can you see things to write, color, and paint with?*

Pages 20–21: *Saws are used to cut things. Can you see something else we use to cut?*

Pages 22–23: *Can you see how the 3 pigs are the same or different from one another?*

Pages 24–25: *Starfish, crabs, and stingrays are all sea animals. Can you see other things that belong in water?*

Pages 26–27: *Where do you think Seymour is going? Where would you go in a boat you made?*

This book is filled with many things to talk about. Turn this book into a favorite by rereading it, inviting your child to say the rhyming words, or making up new rhymes. You and your child may want to make your very own juice box boats!

—Akimi Gibson, Early Childhood Specialist

Walter Wick is the photographer of the I Spy series of books, with more than nine million copies in print. He is author and photographer of *A Drop of Water: A Book of Science and Wonder*, which won the Boston Globe/Horn Book Award for Nonfiction, was named a Notable Children's Book by the American Library Association, and was selected as an Orbis Pictus Honor Book and a CBC/NSTA Outstanding Science Trade Book for Children. *Walter Wick's Optical Tricks*, a book of photographic illusions, was named a Best Illustrated Children's Book by the *New York Times Book Review*, was recognized as a Notable Children's Book by the American Library Association, and received many awards, including a Platinum Award from the Oppenheim Toy Portfolio, a Young Readers Award from *Scientific American*, a *Bulletin* Blue Ribbon, and a Parents' Choice Silver Honor. *Can You See What I See?*, published in 2003, appeared on the *New York Times* Bestseller List for 22 weeks. His most recent book is *Can You See What I See?: Dream Machines*. Mr. Wick has invented photographic games for *GAMES* magazine and photographed covers for books and magazines, including *Newsweek*, *Discover*, and *Psychology Today*. A graduate of Paier College of Art, Mr. Wick lives with his wife, Linda, in New York and Connecticut.